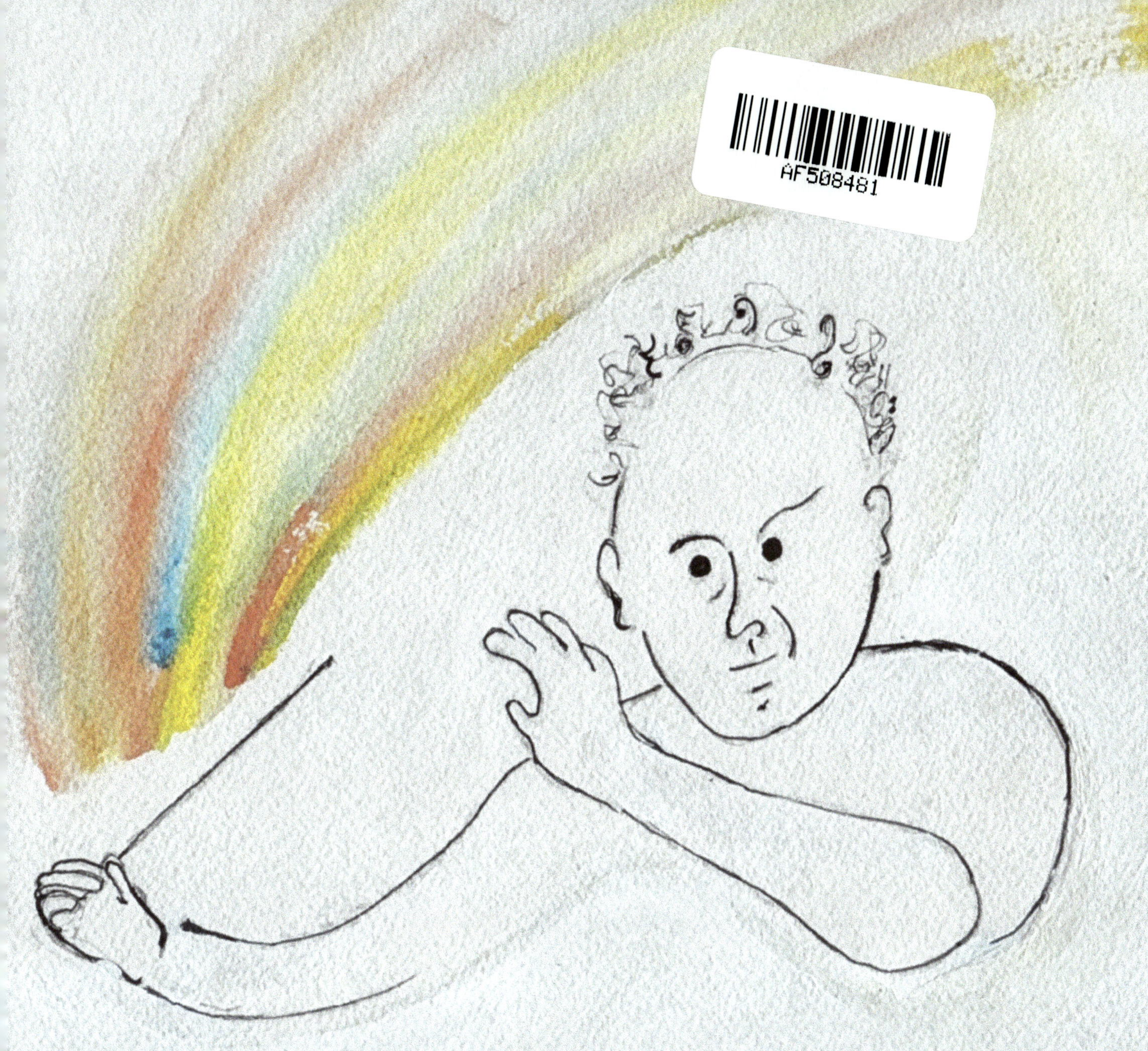

The Orchestra

Stephen Bates

Violin

Like a lark ascending,

She wants to be on

The highest note for

Any ending.

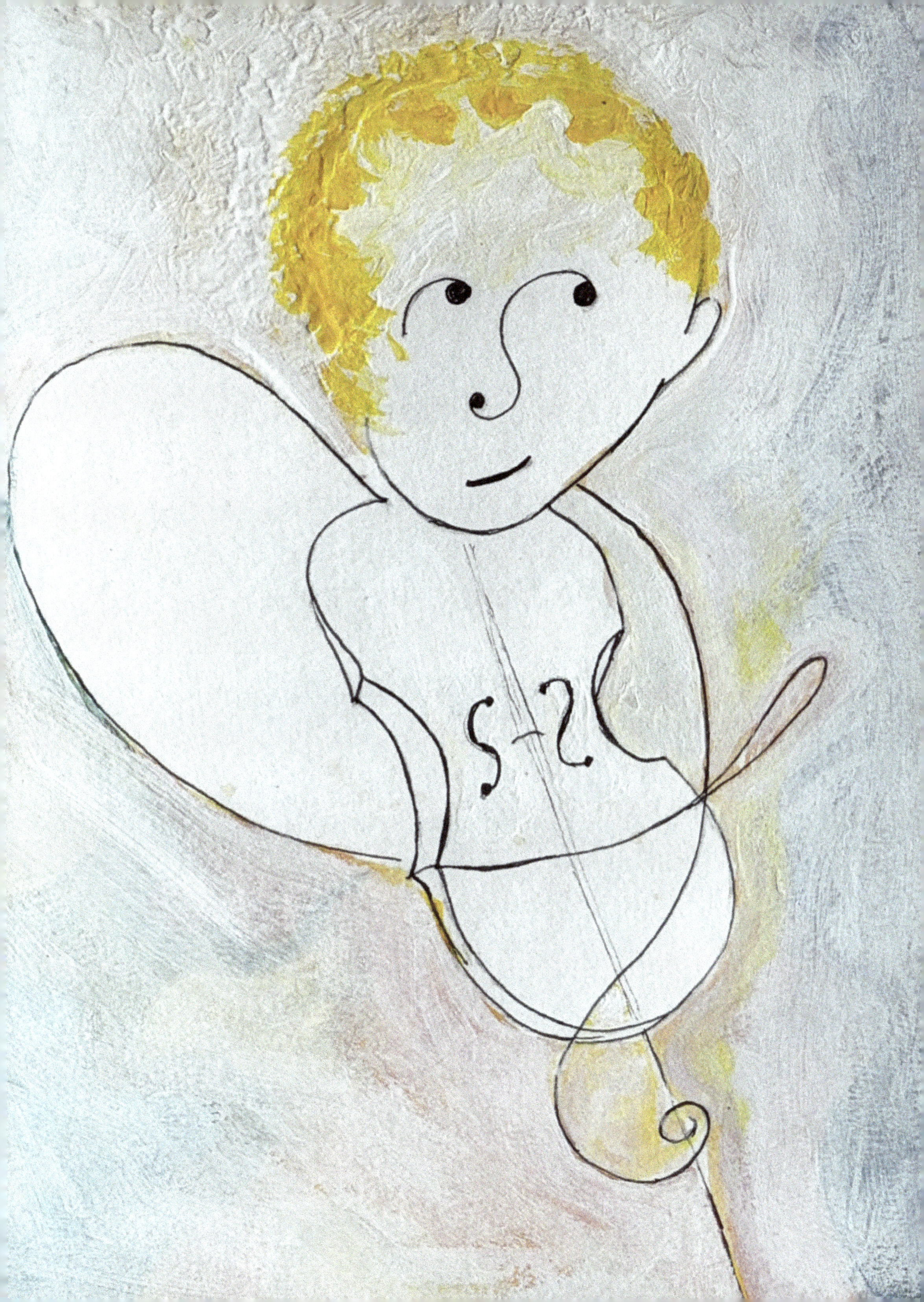

Viola

A sound that tastes

Like a rich red wine,

Vinified with grapes

Ripened on the vine.

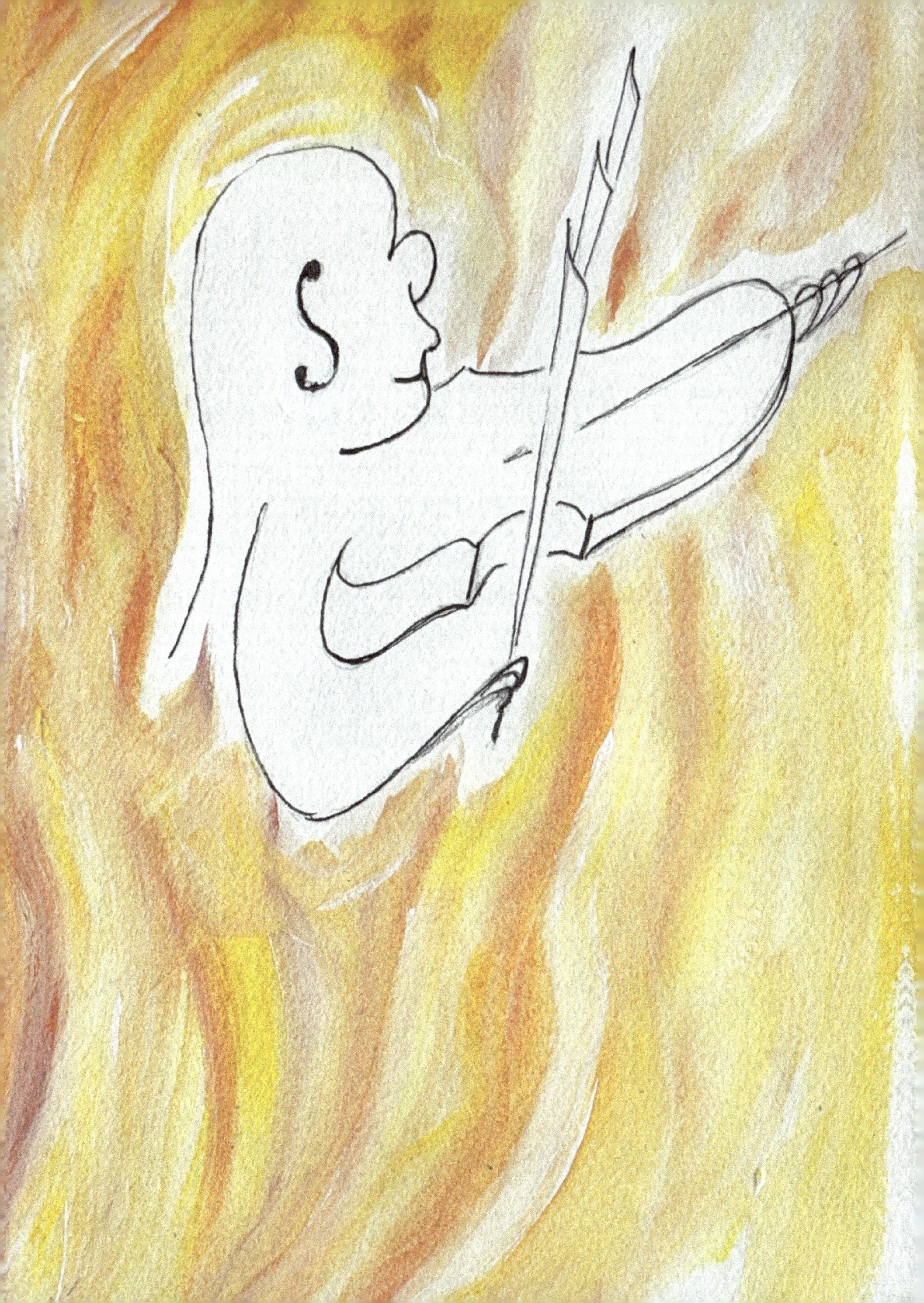

Cello

The cellist and her instrument,

Lovers in a rapture,

The whole audience will capture.

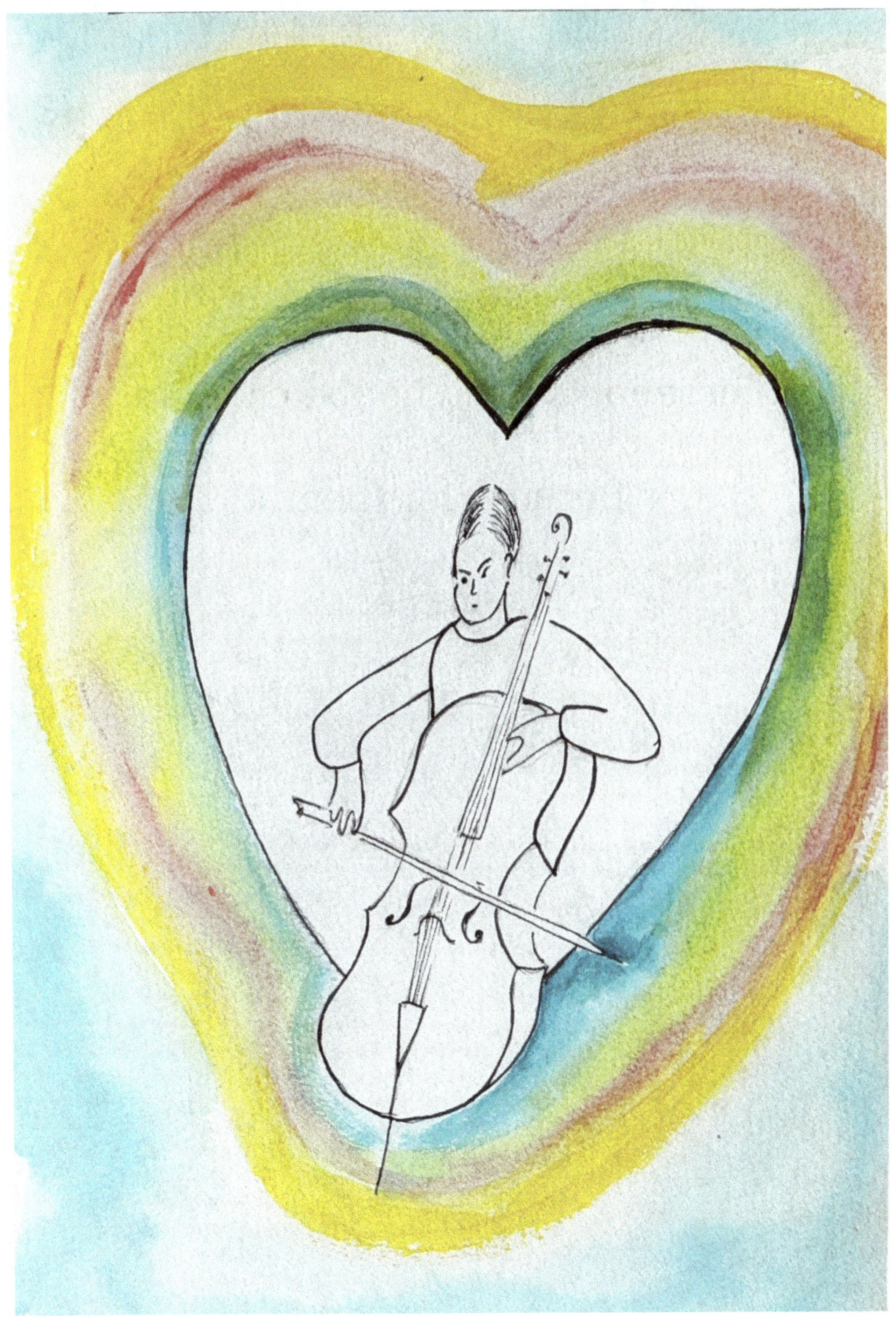

Double Bass

These folks need not be chatters,

Because for them,

Size matters.

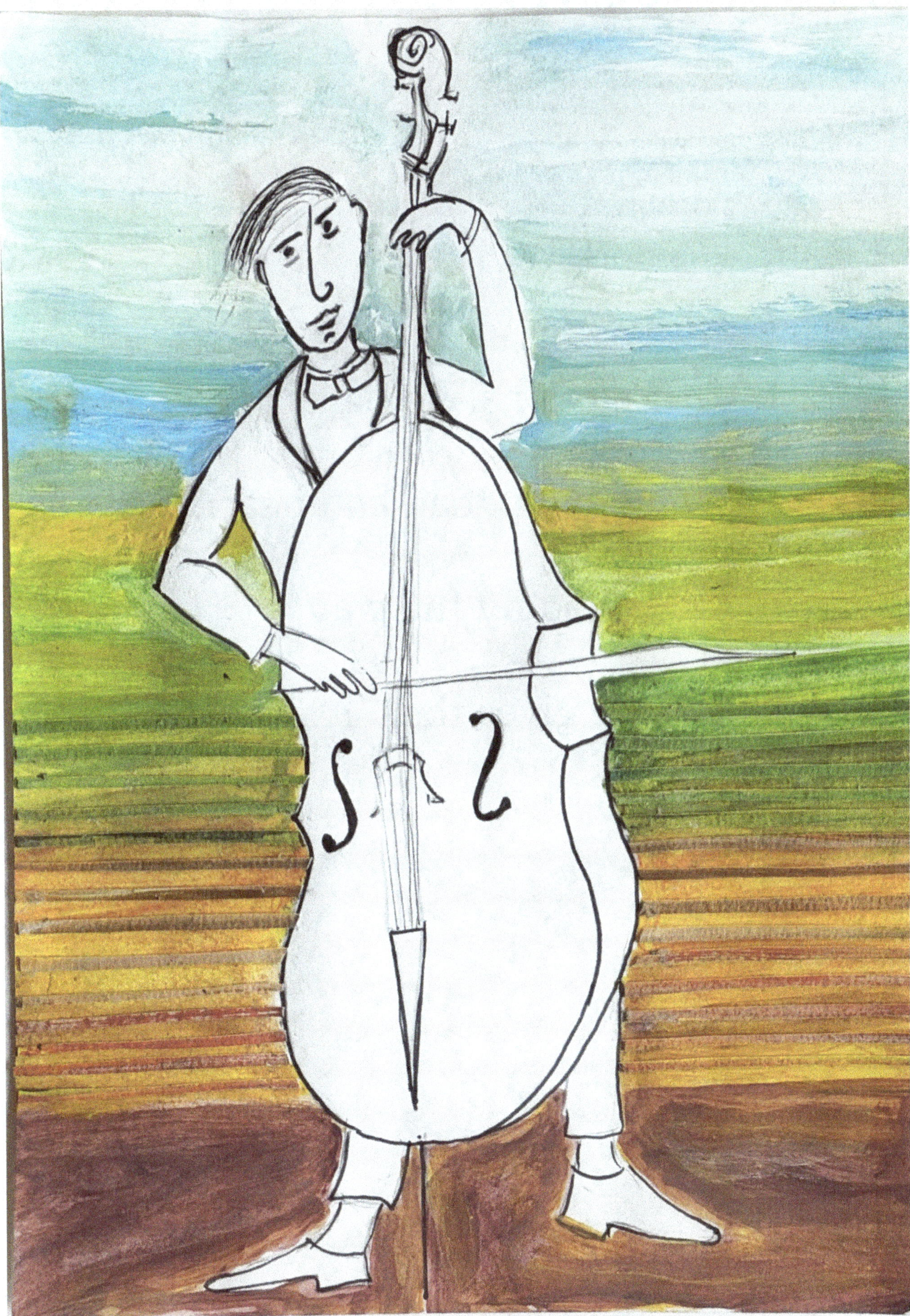

Oboe

Emotional yet smart,

Combining head and heart,

And by the way,

He gives the "A."

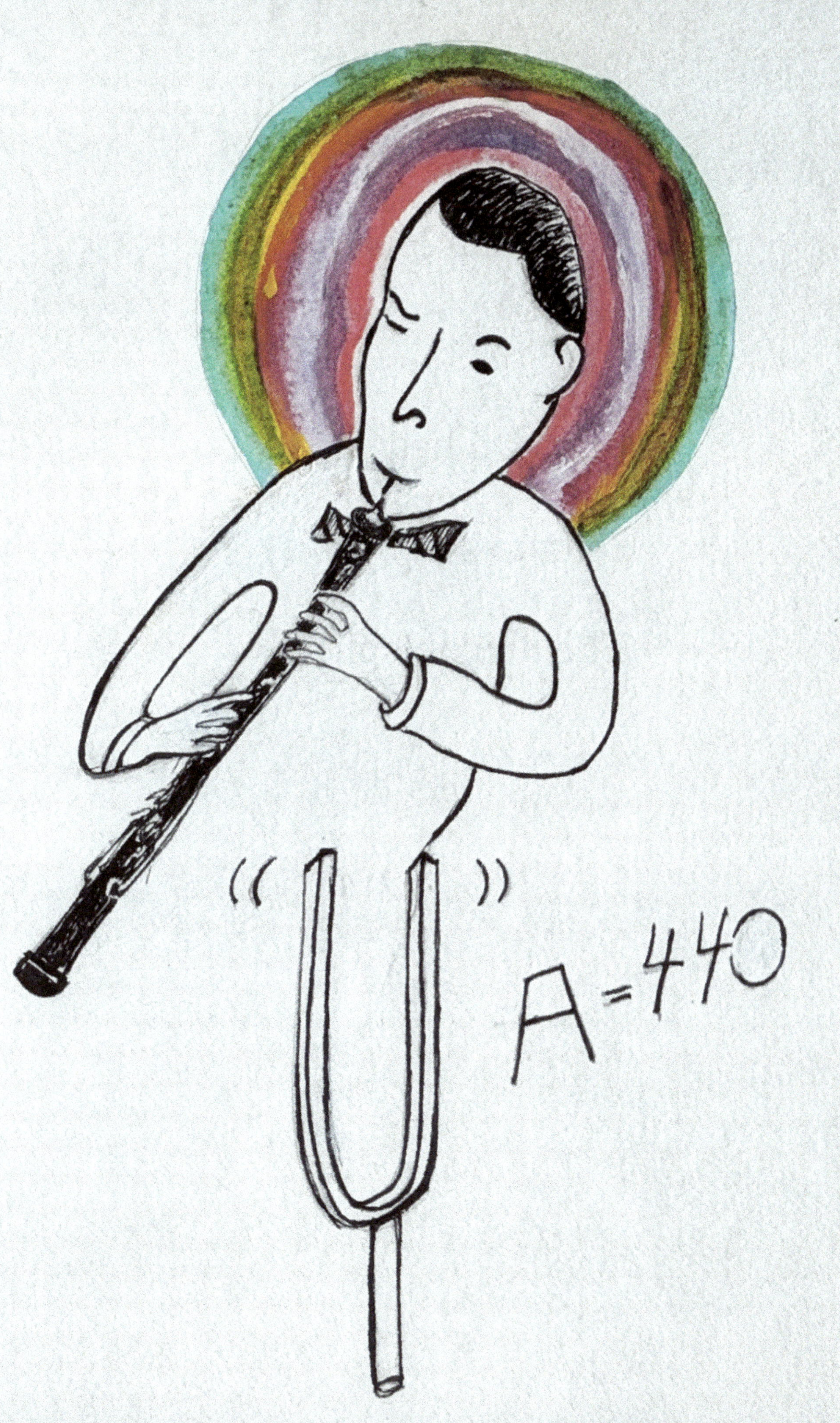
A=440

English Horn

Just to hear it

Connects you with

The human spirit.

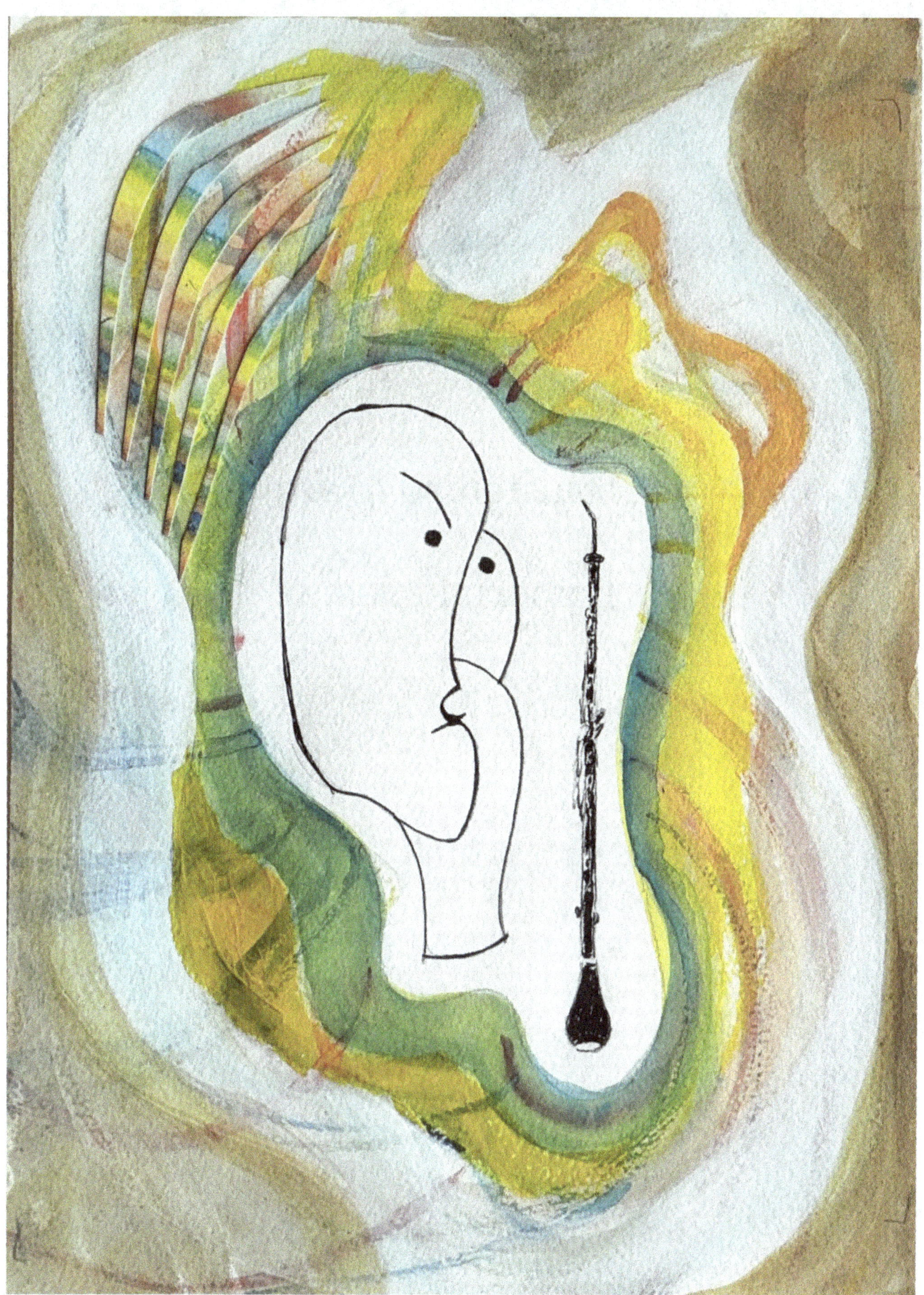

Flute

Floating above the rest,

Accustomed to an

Immortal quest.

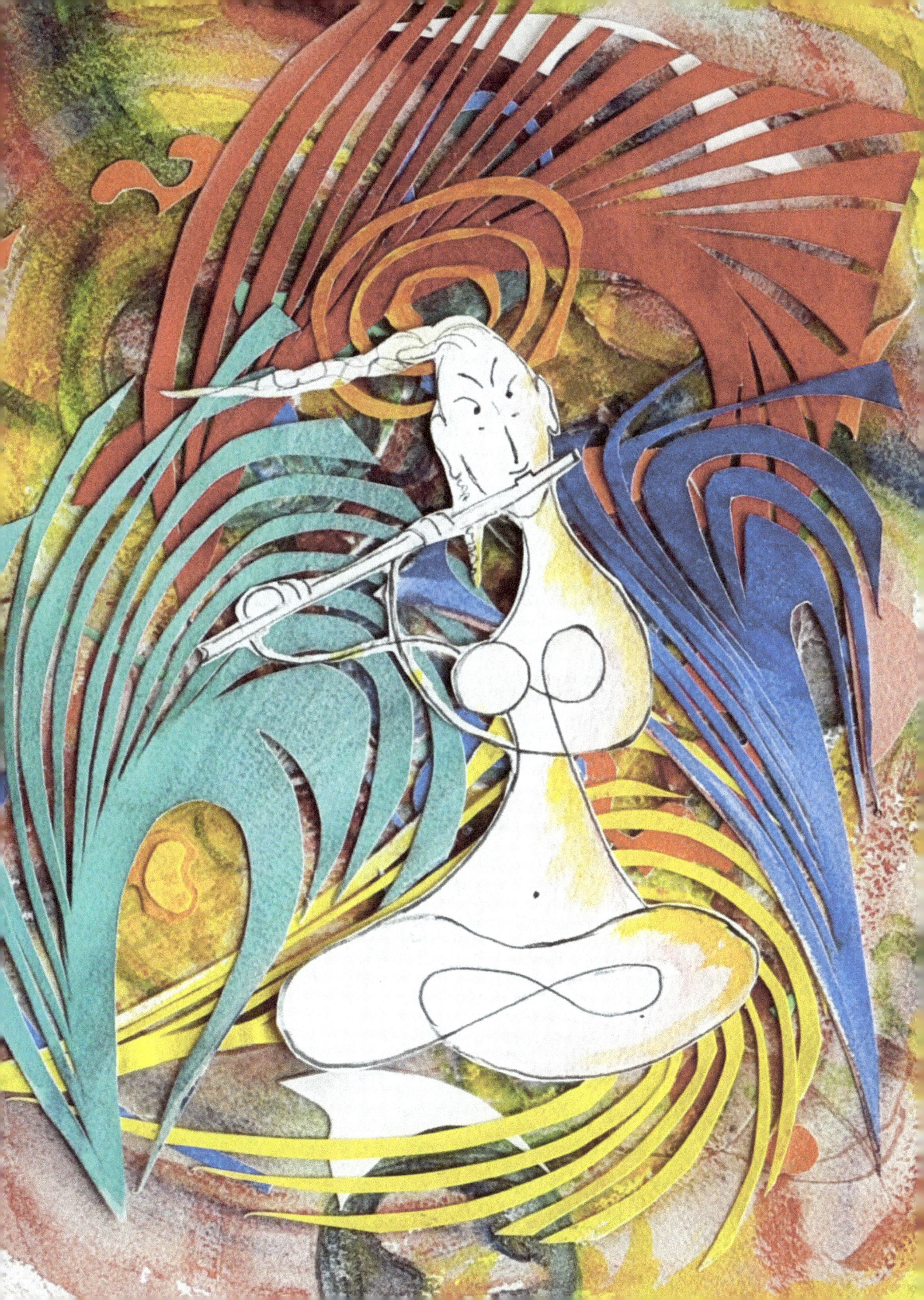

Piccolo

Even on a rainy day,

When you hear the piccolo,

You just want to go out and play!

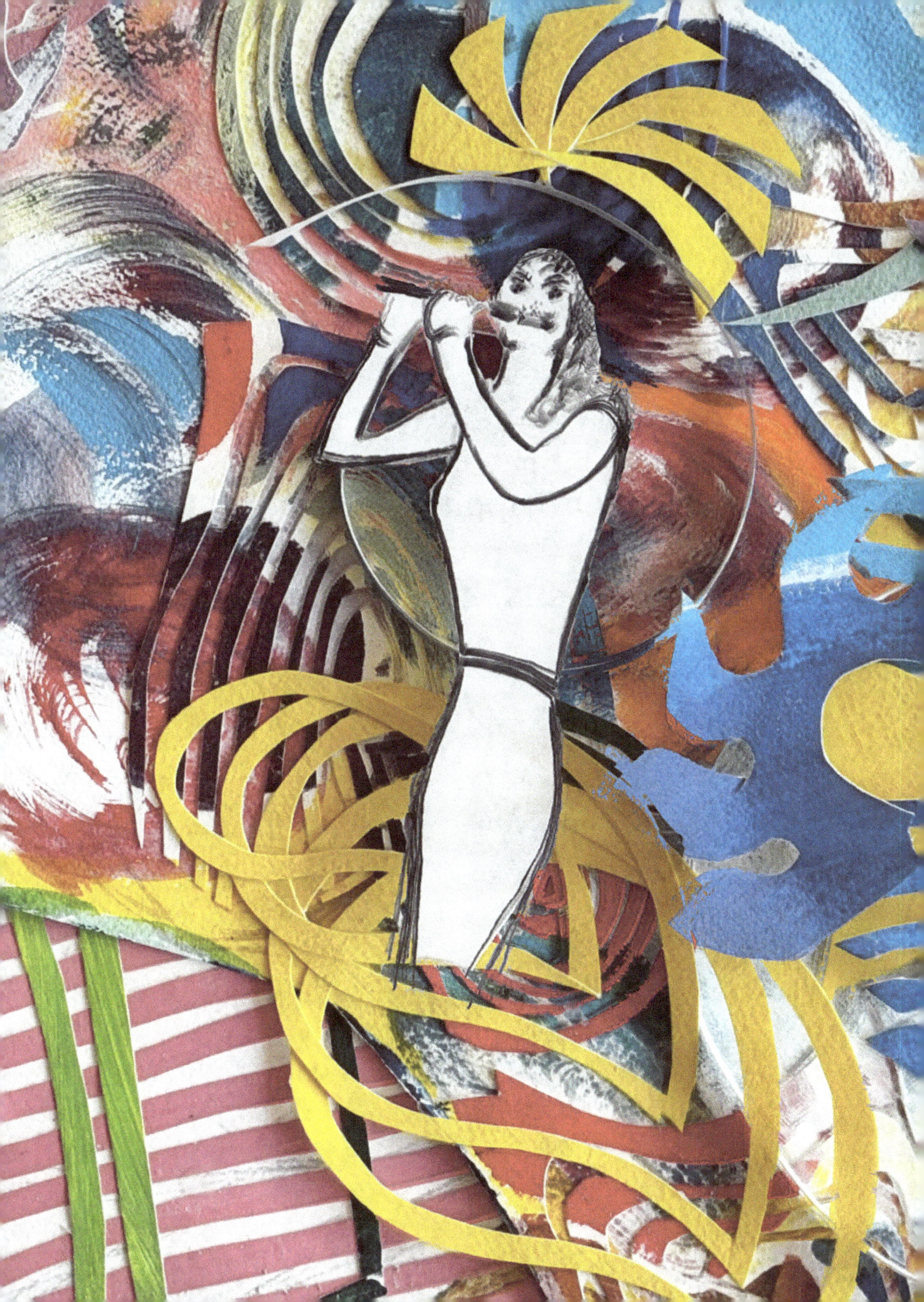

Clarinet

A sound that can be sad

Or trippingly glad,

In the end, always a friend.

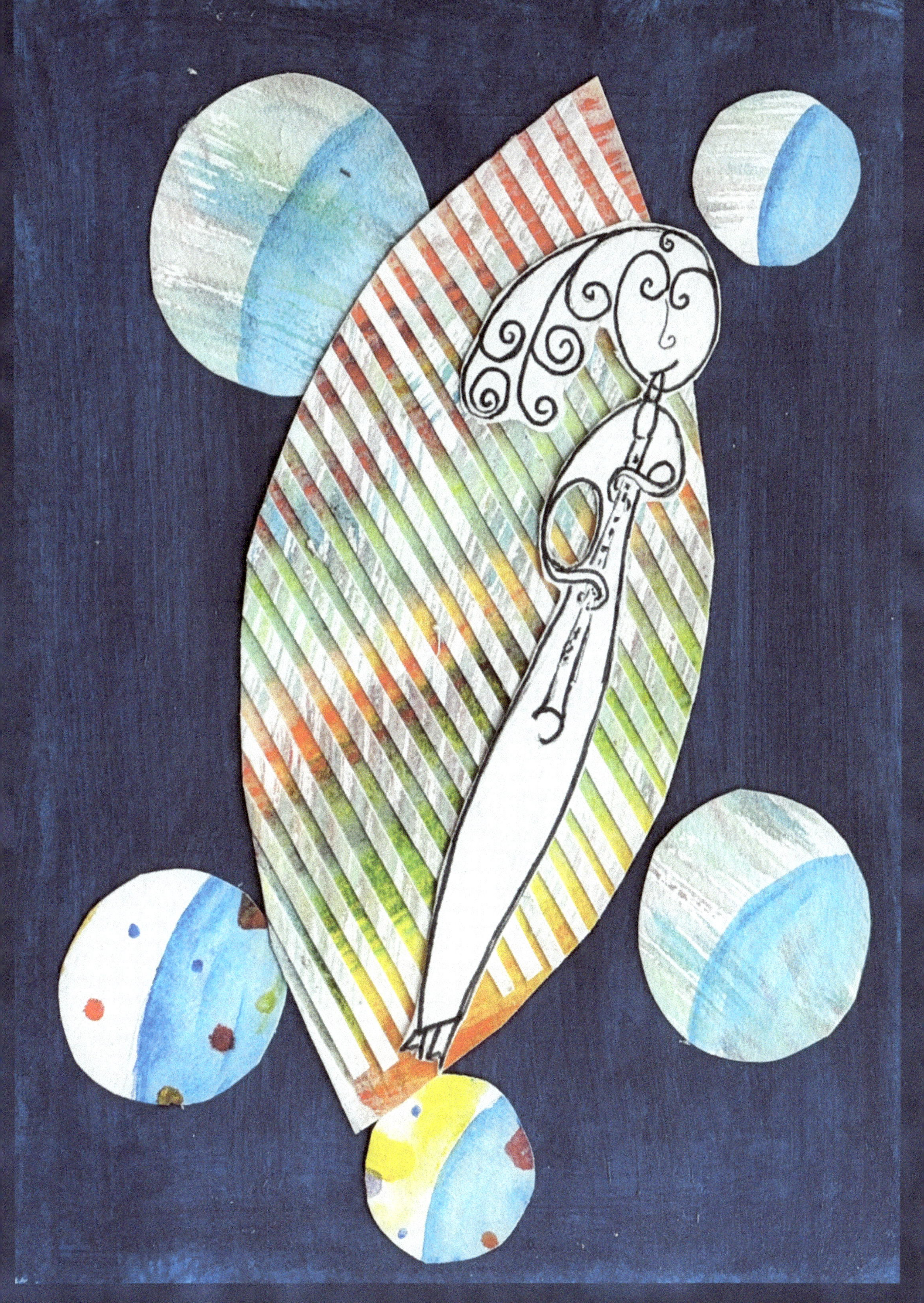

Bass Clarinet

A bit anonymous,

Often ominous,

Expressing moments hard to abide,

Portraying our shadow side.

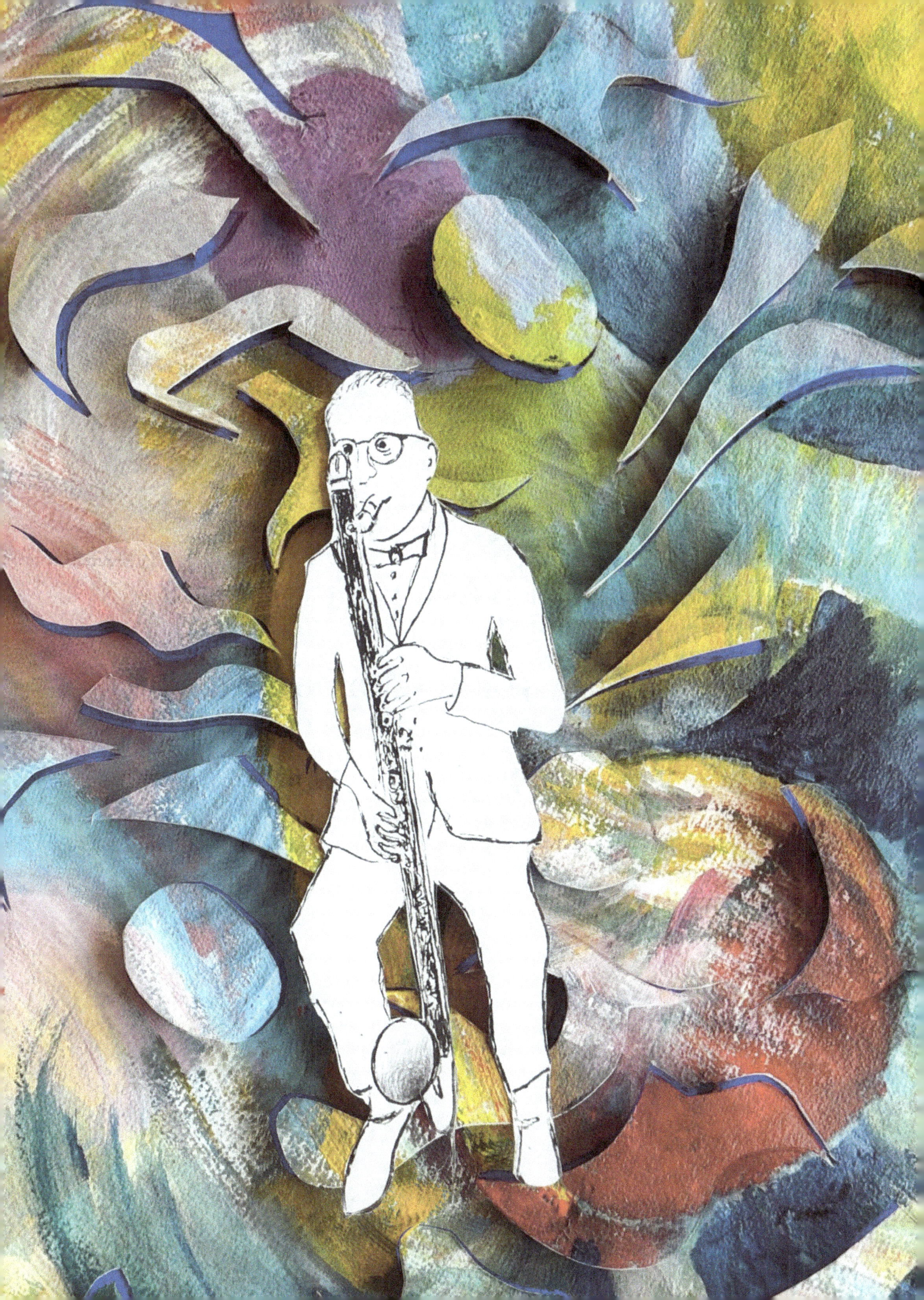

Eb Clarinet

It penetrates throughout

The concert hall

As much as any other.

To play it, you can't hide behind

The apron of your mother.

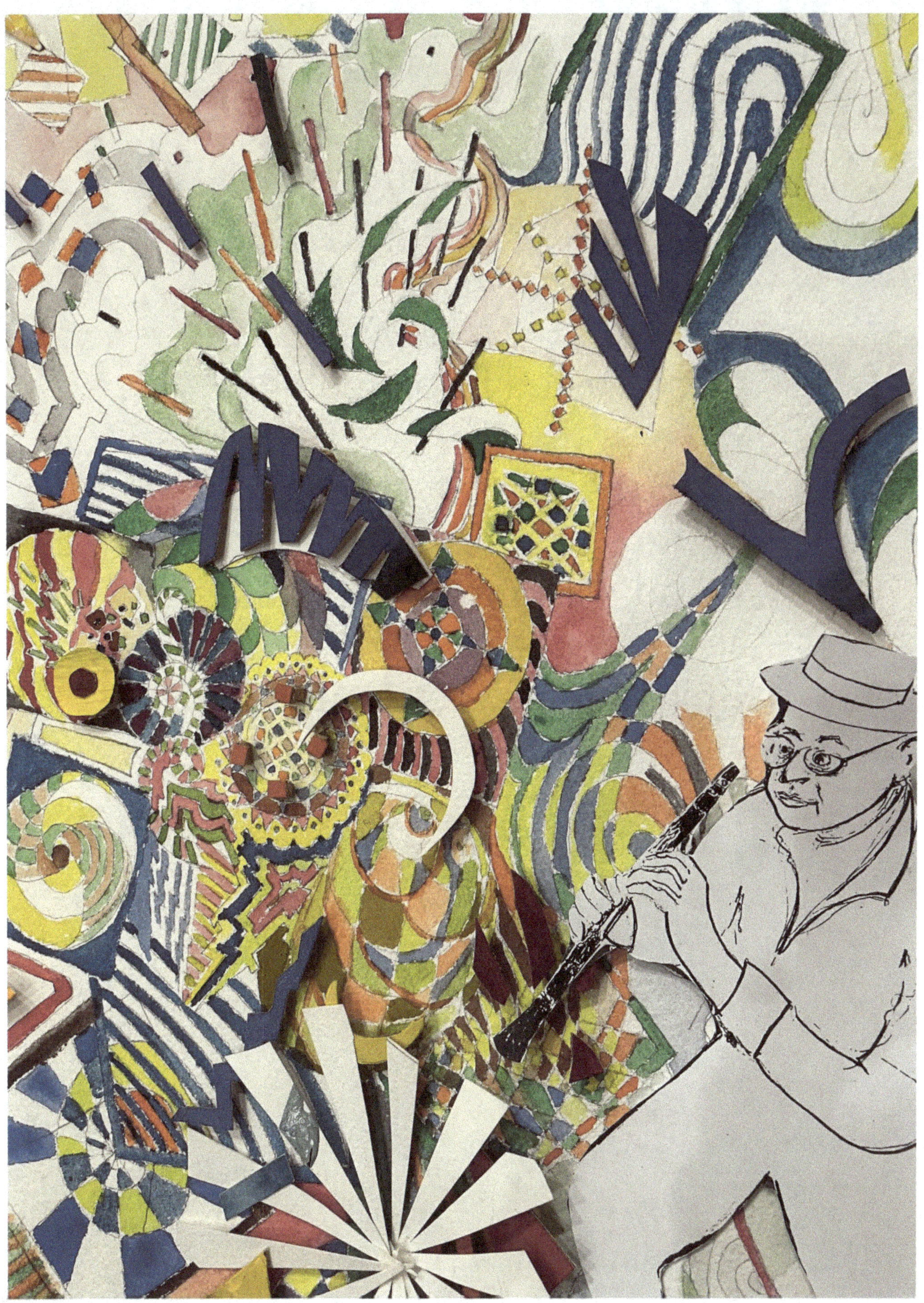

Bassoon

Interested in cosmology,

Expert in psychology,

And with no apology, like

Enjoying a sweet confection,

Has a taste for perfection.

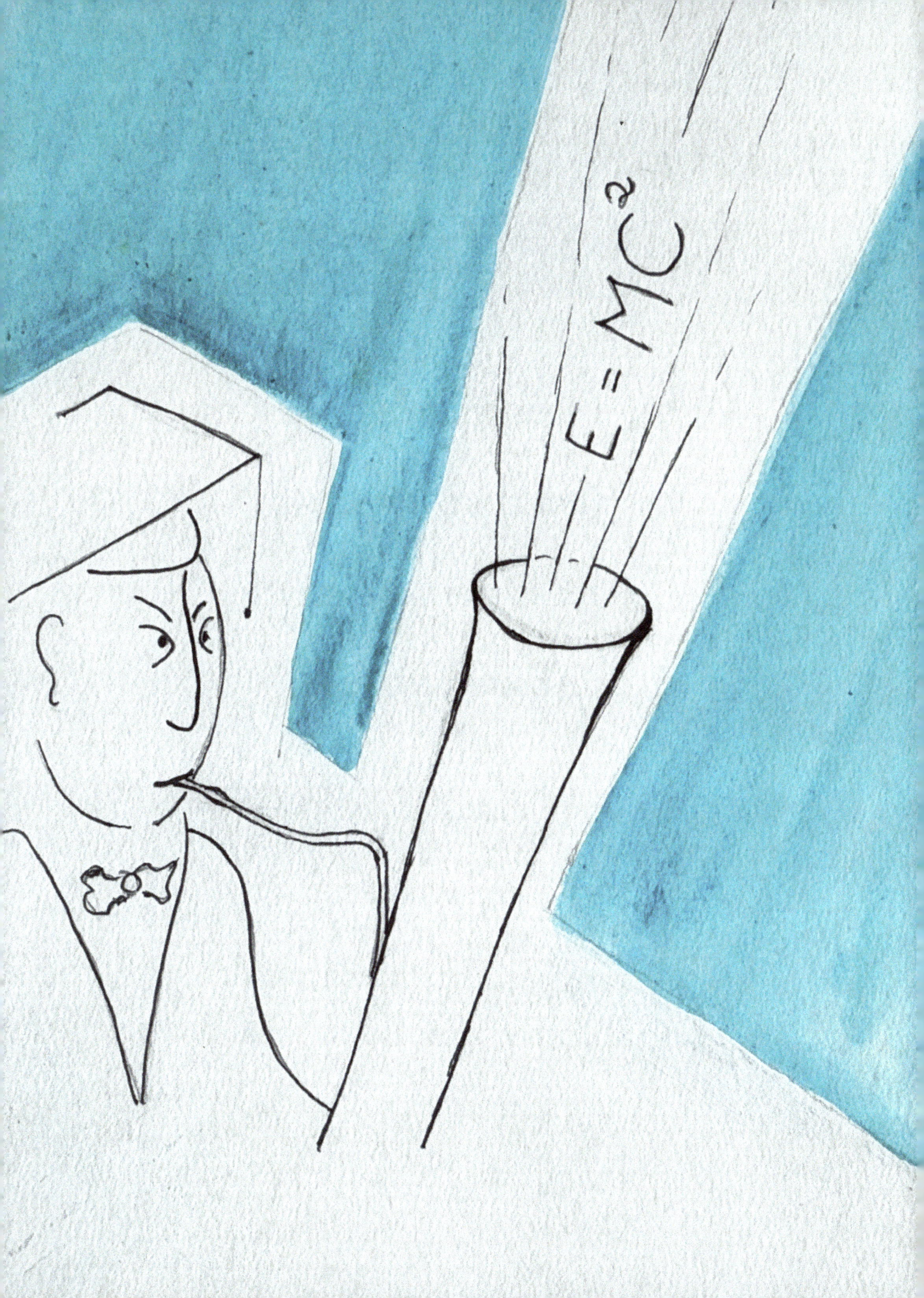

E = MC²

Contra Bassoon

It has a sound like a deep rattle,

(not from a snake)

Rather from the earth

About to quake!

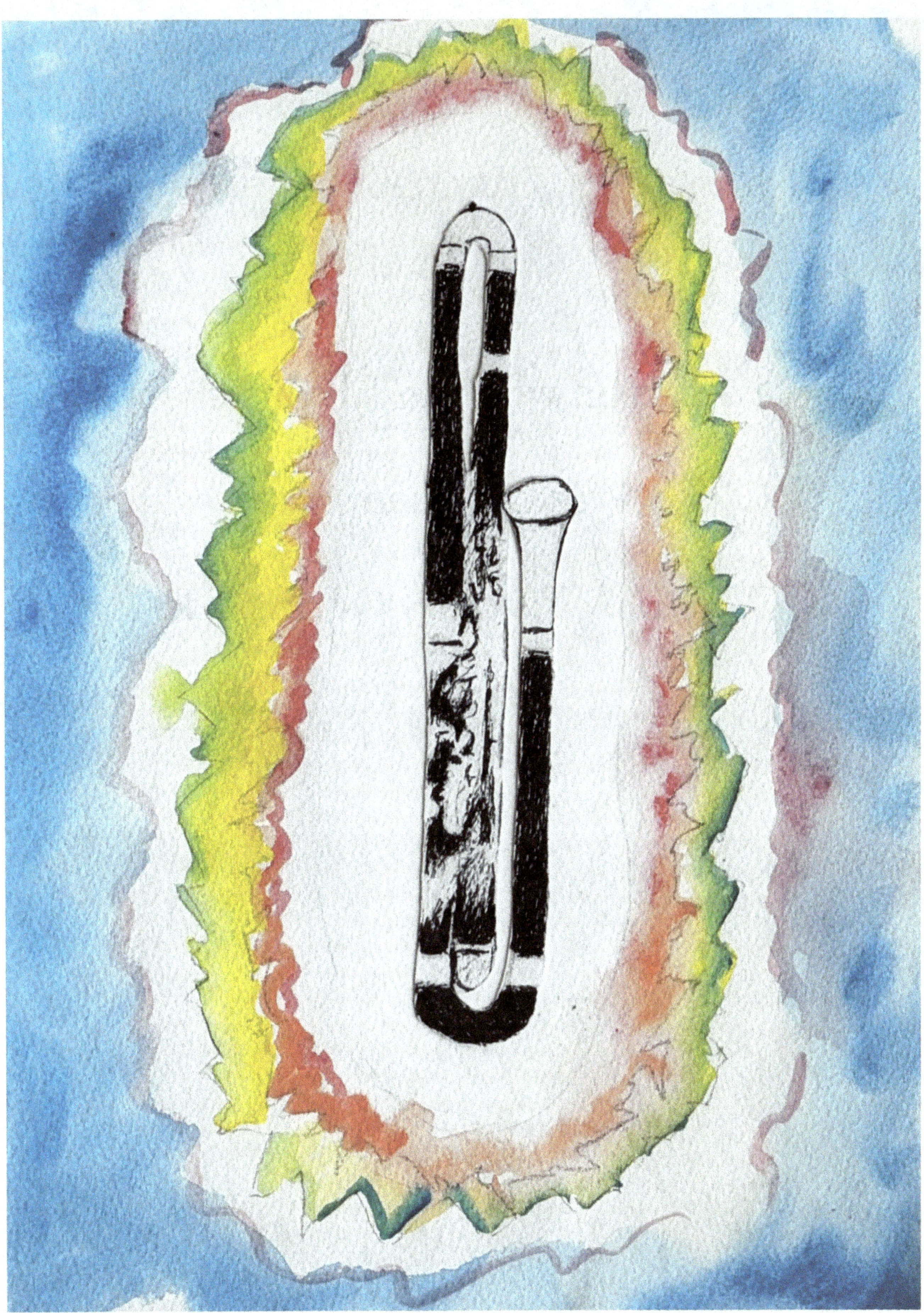

Trumpet

The person who can fill this chair

Is confident

WITH A TOUCH OF FLAIR

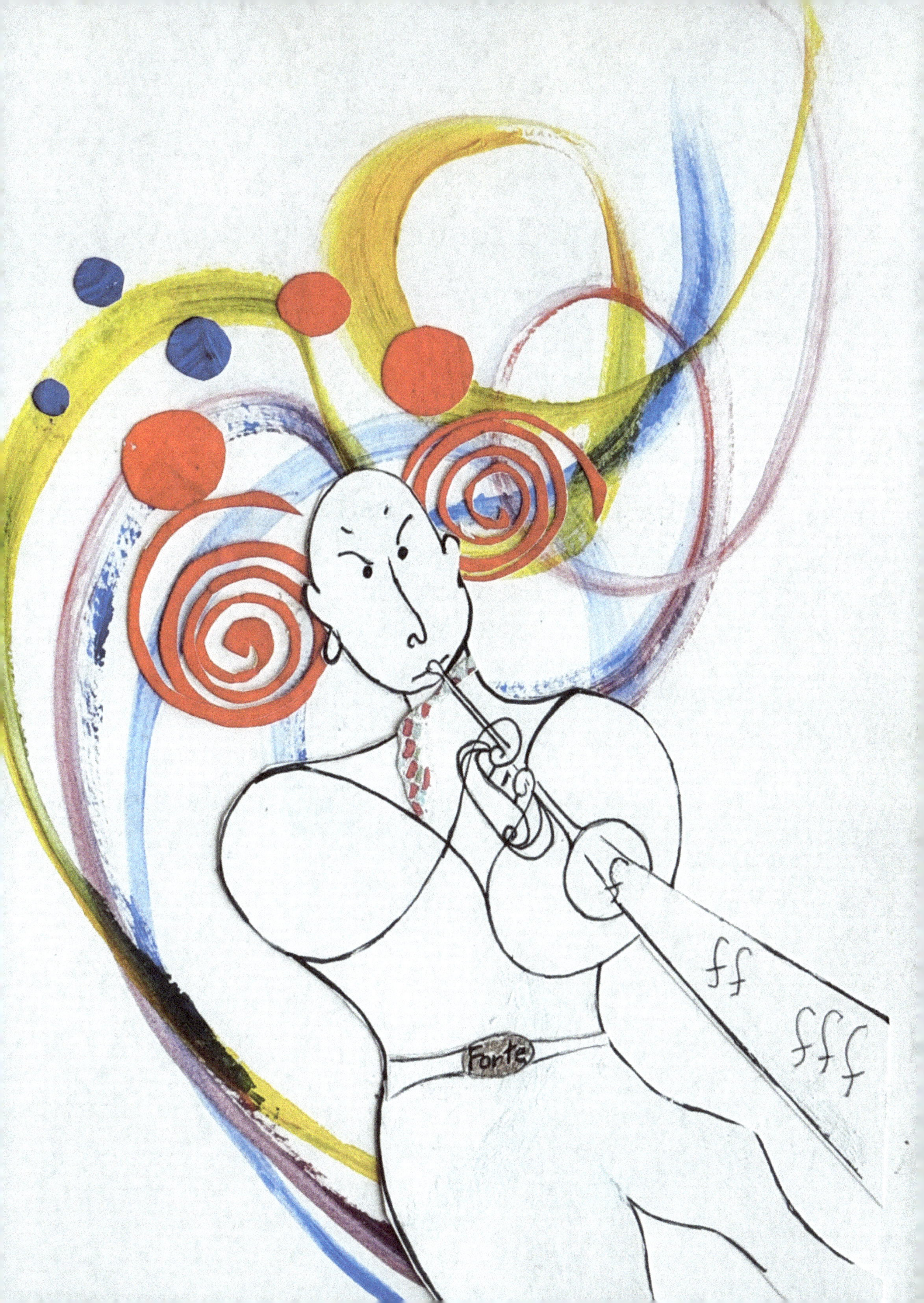
Forte
ff
fff

Trombone

With their characteristic slide,

They help the orchestra to glide.

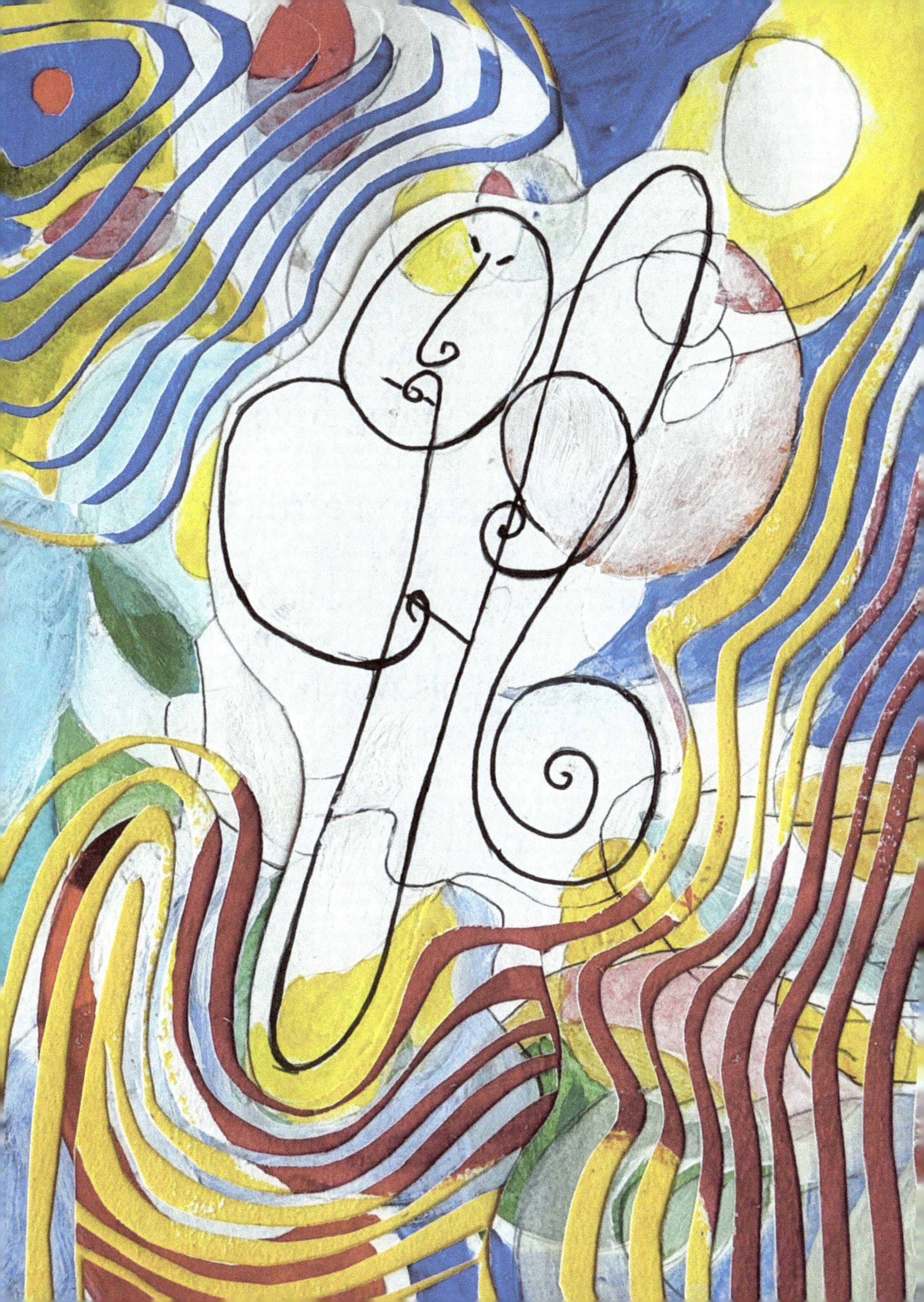

Tuba

A sound coming from

Deep within the earth,

Played by a musician

For all his worth.

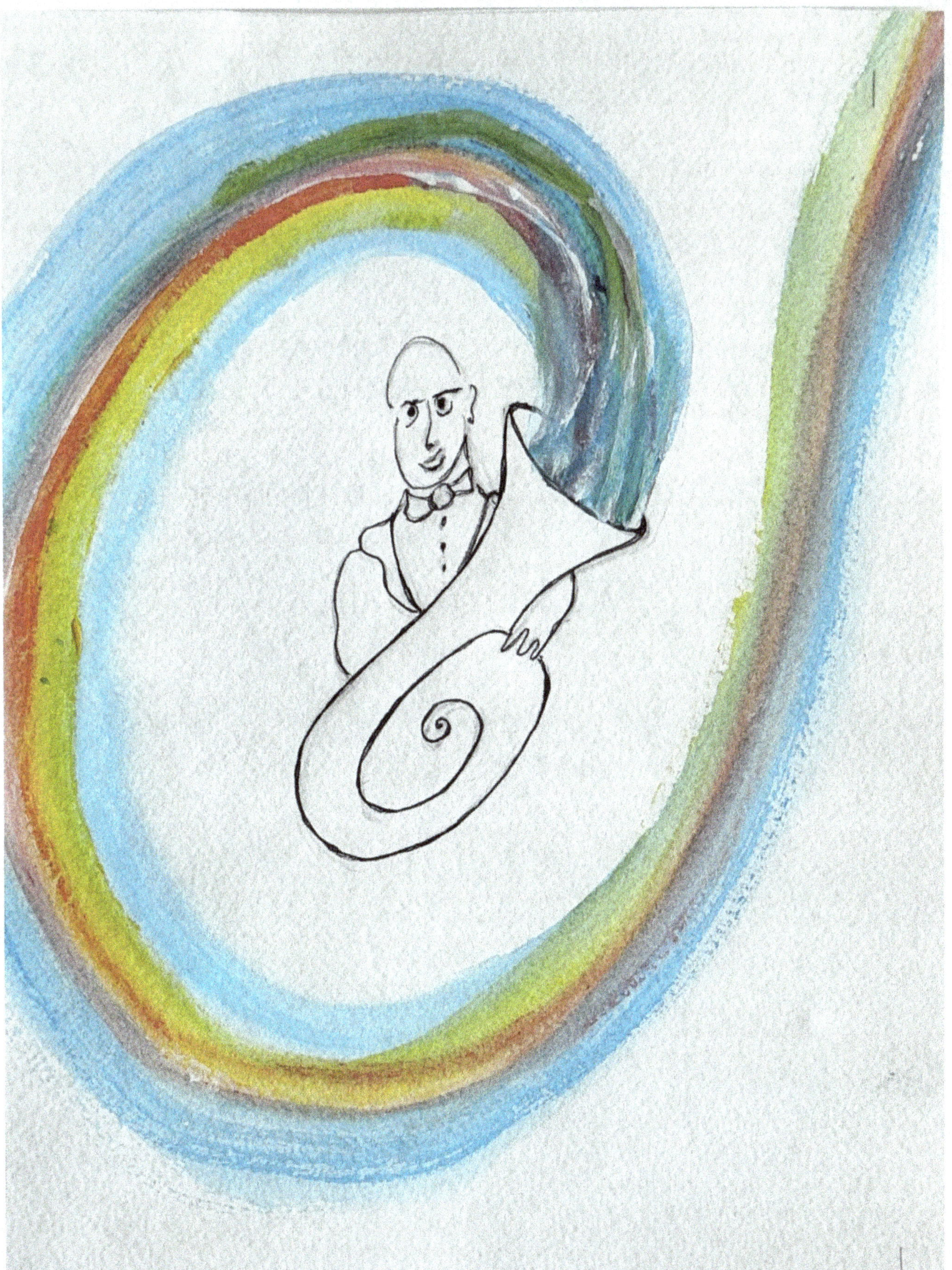

French Horn

Every instrument wants to share

A moment playing with the horns,

Walking on air.

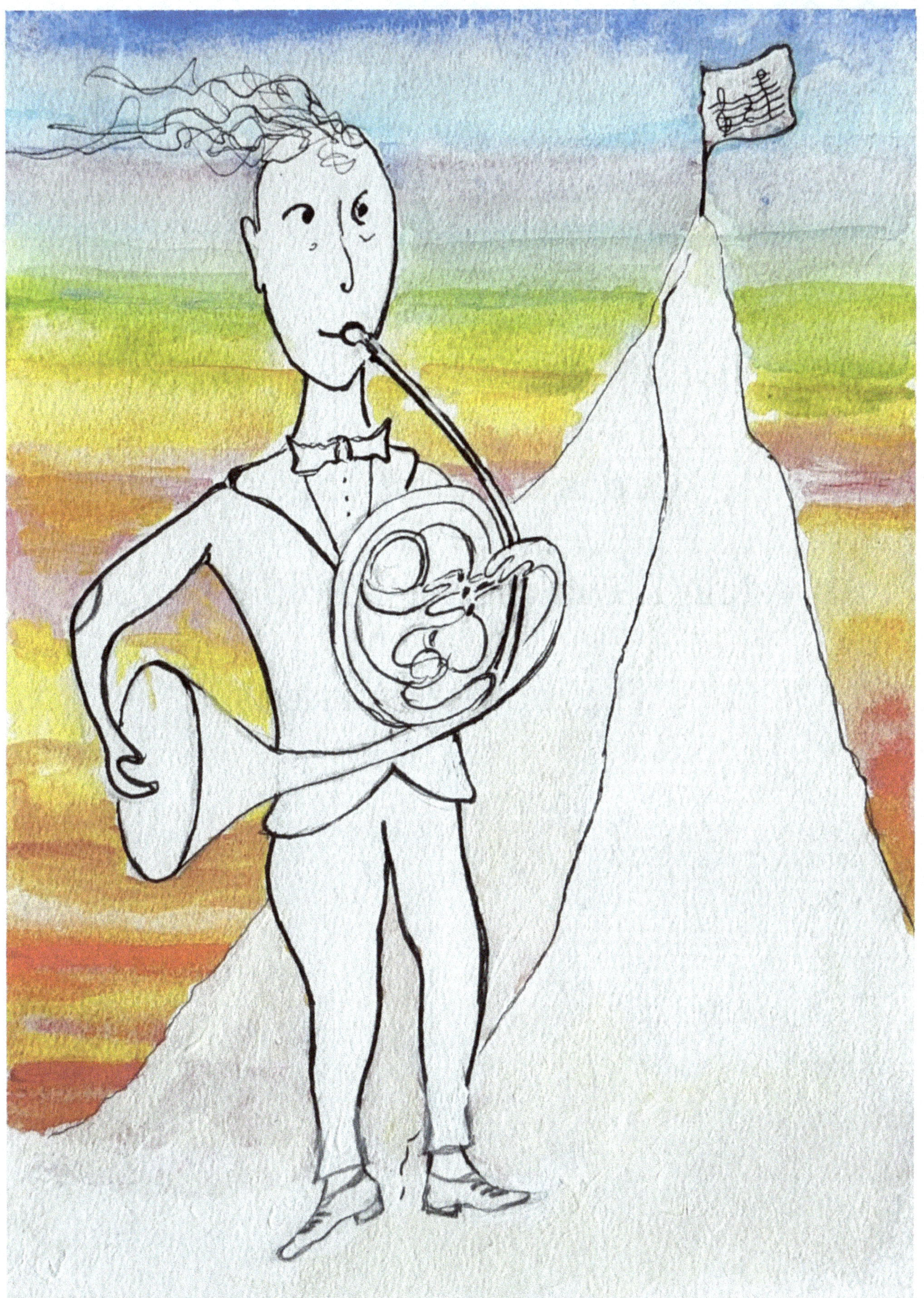

Harp

Whether modern or ancient relic,

Harp is the most angelic.

As young David comforted old King Saul,

The modern version

Soothes us all.

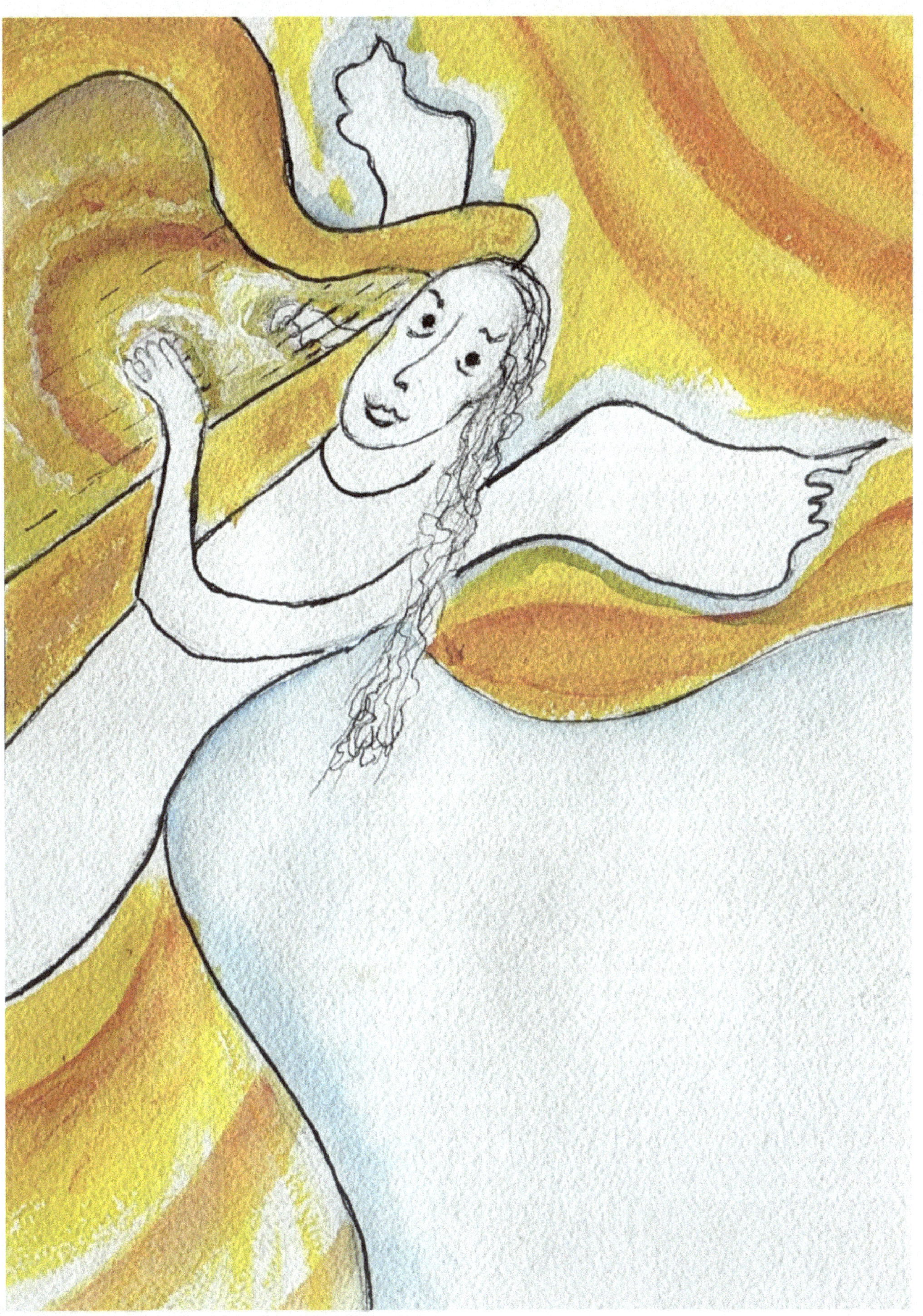

Timpani

Shiva armed symphonist,

The versatile timpanist,

Engenders calm or

Blistering rage.

This musician

Sets the stage.

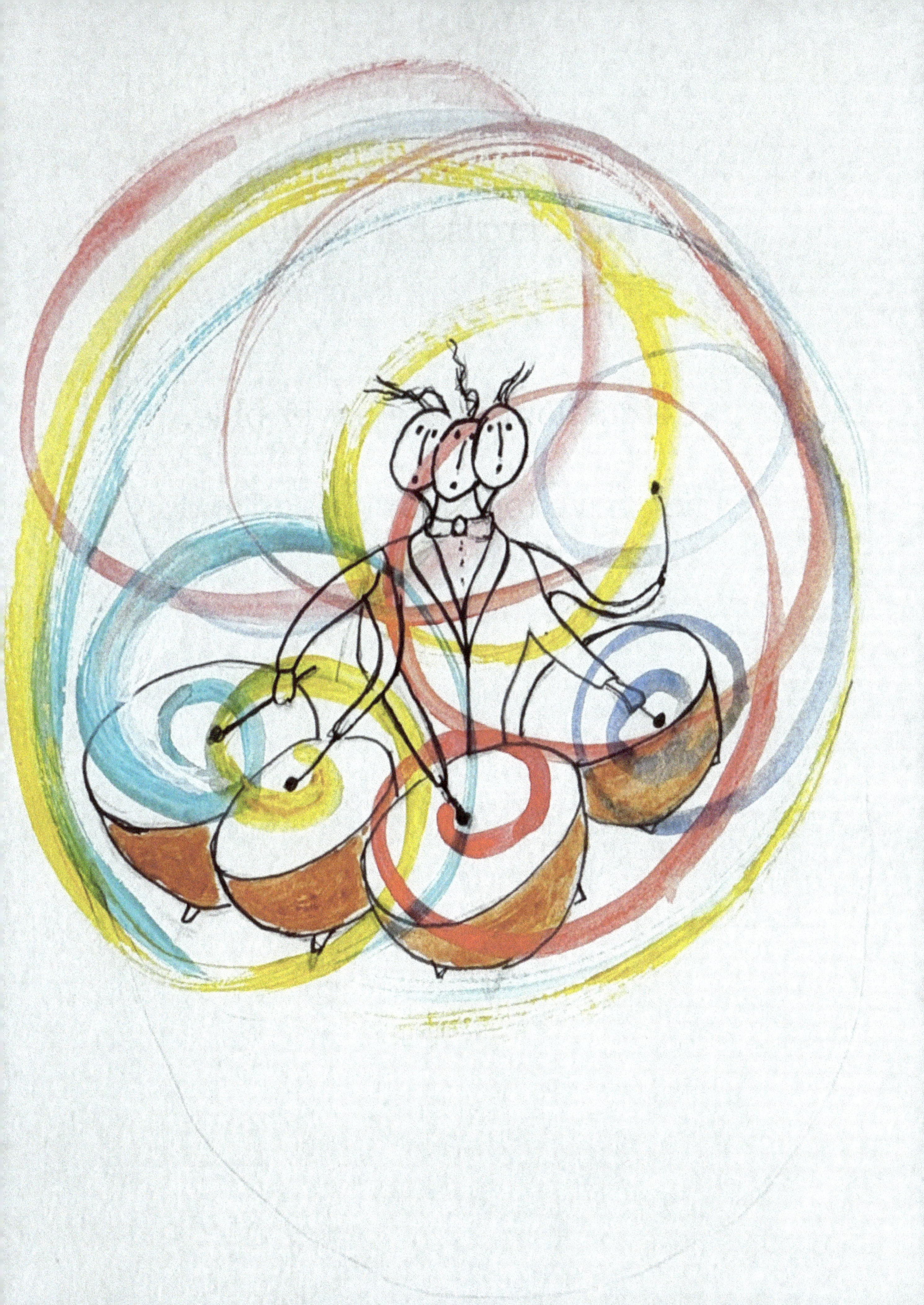

The Percussion Section

Percussionists are never blue,

They have too many things to do.

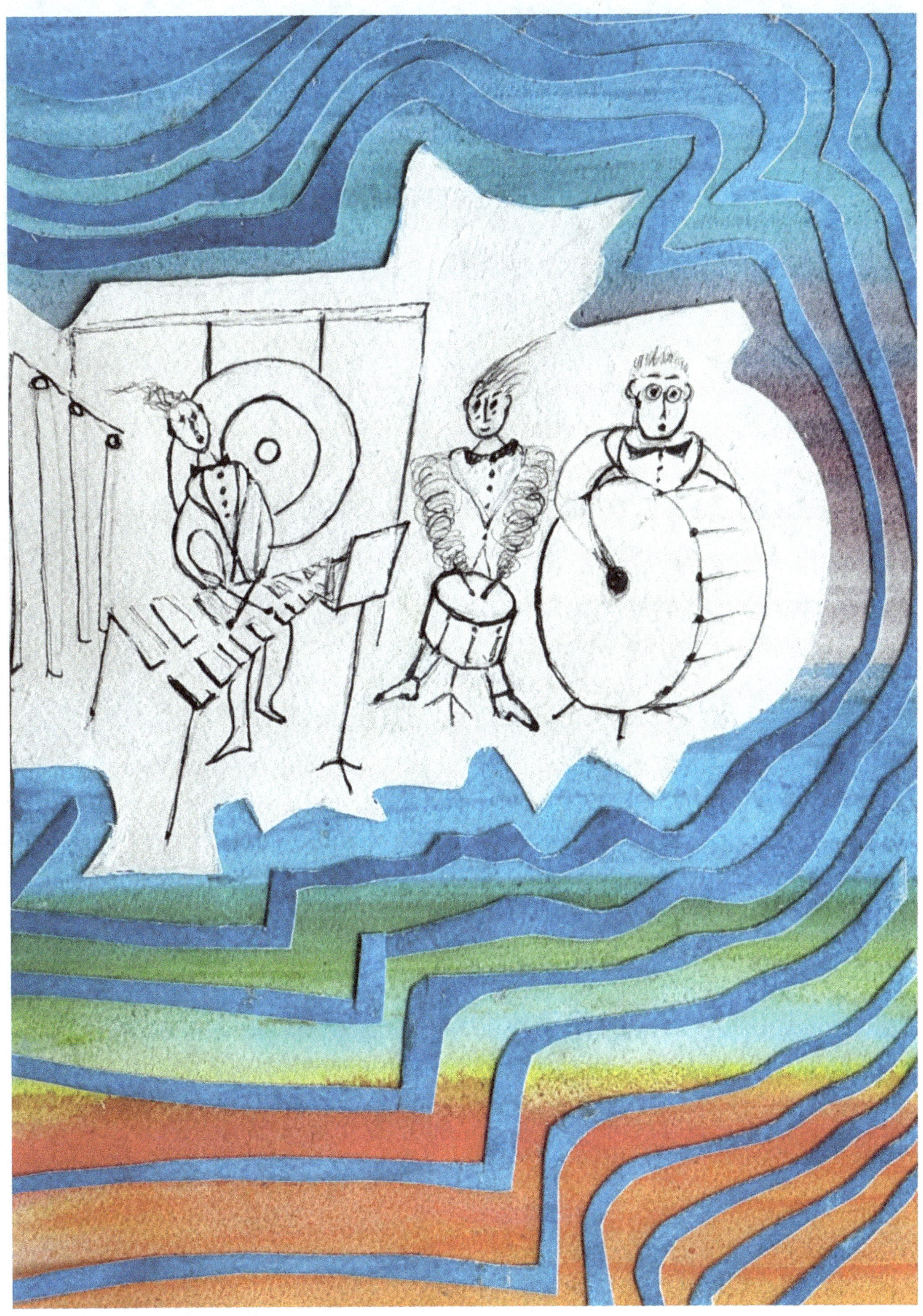

The Orchestral Pianist

On any given day

She may not have too much to play,

However, every note in your ear will stay.

With her extra time she can

Read a lot of books,

Which draws from jealous colleagues

A lot of dirty looks.

It can't be said she isn't well read!

James Joyce
Copland
Shostakovitch
Vogue
Stravinsky

The Conductor

His instrument is a small baton

With which he

Makes the show go on.

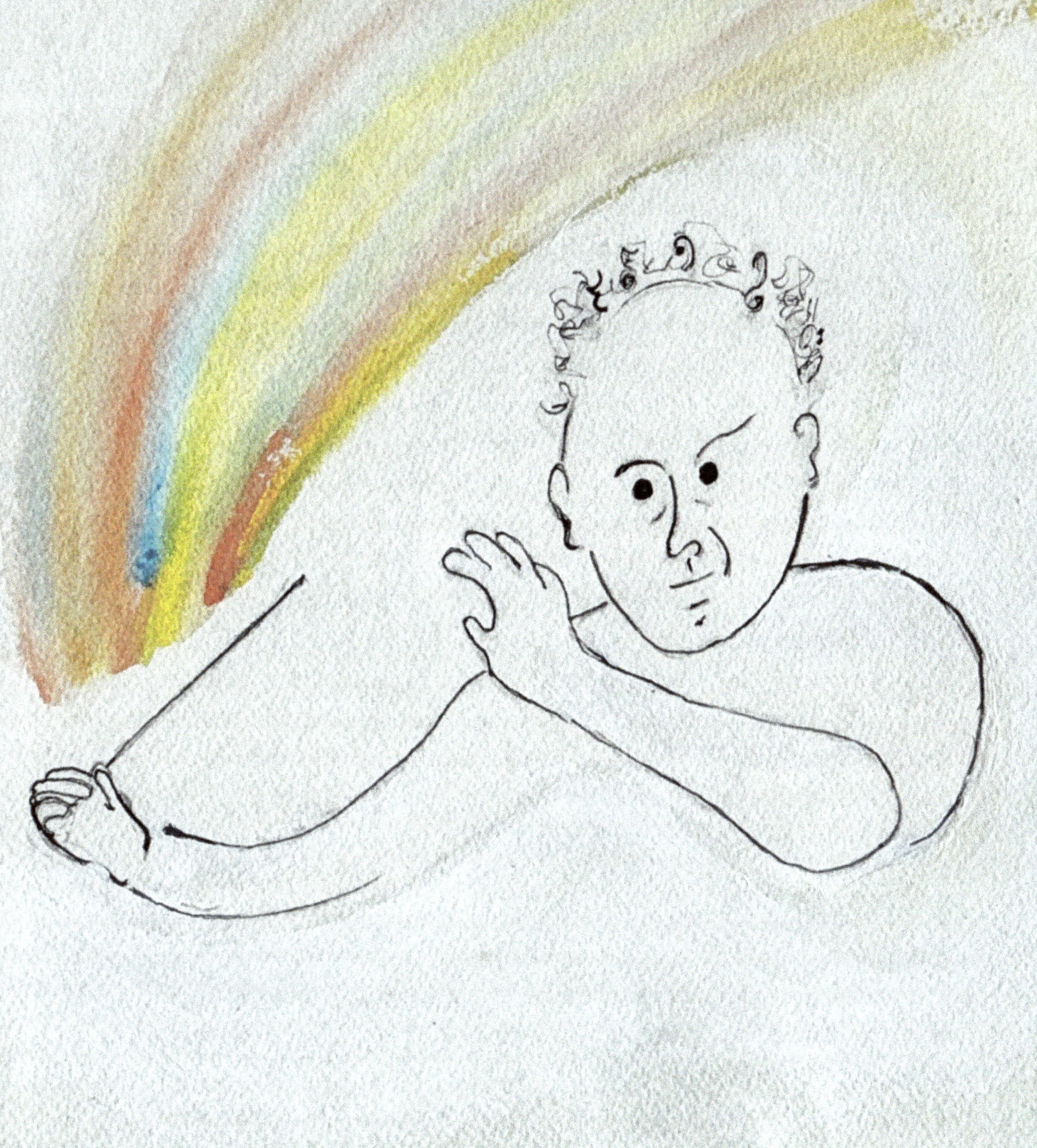

Music, Art, and Me

I grew up in a small town, Patchogue, Long Island. Mister Rosen, who owned the local music store, played saxophone and clarinet. At six years old, I was walking around in their house and came upon an open closet. There, out of their cases and leaning on the walls, were a saxophone and a clarinet. So overwhelming was the image of the silver keys of the clarinet and the brass saxophone with its pearl covered keys. I thought, who can manage this stuff?

At ten years old, I started playing clarinet, imitating Mr. Rosen's son, Joe, who was four years older. At twelve my father took me to hear the New York Philharmonic. After the concert, we went back to see Mr. Bernstein. My father told him that I was a musician. Bernstein looked me over and said, "You play clarinet." Is it because I was thin, quiet, shy?

Does the child choose the instrument or the other way around?

At fourteen, again following the lead of Joe Rosen, I went to Red Fox Music Camp. On the first day, when I wandered into the music barn, four counselors were playing a quartet by Ralph Vaughan Williams. I had never seen anything like this. Four grown men playing classical music open heartedly, exposing their love for the music. After that summer, I asked my father to get me a real clarinet teacher.

The one my father found refused. "No," he said, "he has to study with Leon Russianoff." So we visited Mr. Russianoff in New York City, 48th St. and Broadway. Russianoff said I should study with his student, Jack Kreiselman, who had a studio down the hall.

I took the two-hour train ride from Patchogue to NYC every Saturday for four years. After I had worked with Kreiselman for a year, Russianoff accepted me as his student. Mr. Russianoff gave me the foundation for clarinet playing, and to this day I play always wanting to come up to the level that he expected. He was both a great clarinet teacher and a friendly, enormously inspiring presence.

I got my first playing job in the United States Marine Band, a four-year enlistment. This band played at the White House. We performed for Lyndon Johnson and Richard Nixon and saw many celebrities come and go. I'll never forget the time Duke Ellington sat down at the piano, the bass player and drummer joining in. Was Ellington suggesting that the White House is a big deal, but music is still the greatest thing there is?

In 1973, I joined the almost-brand-new Kennedy Center, with the fledgling Opera House Orchestra, performing for opera and ballets. I played with that orchestra for thirty-six years, playing in seventy different opera productions and over four hundred performances of the Nutcracker Suite.

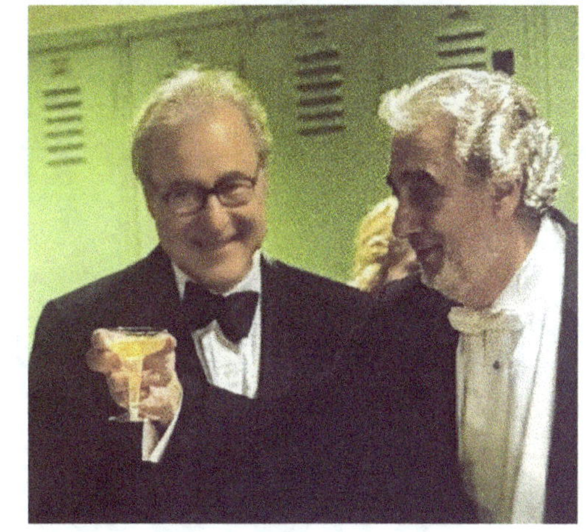

Since operatic literature is focused on telling a human story, moods shift wildly. Opera orchestra players need to be on their toes all the time to go with the changes. This is great training for any musician. I had the opportunity to play some very significant solos in Wagner operas, including Tristan. In an opera by Verdi, I played a bass clarinet solo accompanying Placido Domingo singing on stage.

In 2008, after my last Nutcracker at the Kennedy Center, I gathered together my closest friends including a new member, who that evening was playing her first Nutcracker. When I opened a bottle of champagne, first clarinetist David Jones remarked, "This is the passing on of the Nutcracker soul."

Throughout my years in the orchestra I was also painting and had exhibitions at the Watergate Gallery and the Norman Parish Gallery, both in Washington, D.C. I did not have formal study as a painter, but spent countless hours at the Phillips Collection, one of Washington's greatest treasures.

I learned much from the gallery and got to know its curator, James McLaughlin. This quiet man, himself an accomplished artist, taught me much. When a friend of mine asked him, "What are galleries for?" Jim answered, "They are a place where people can meet." Museums and concert halls bring people together, forging a society that thrives on the highest possible vision for humanity.

After retiring I moved with my wife, Isabella, a singer and meditation teacher, to Manchester, Massachusetts. We have two children. Matthew is an oil painter in Florence, Italy, and Jessica is an actress in New York City. I continue to paint and make art, and to play clarinet in home concerts.

This time in my life has been an opportunity to expand as an artist and clarinetist, to relish more time with friends and family, and, through this book, to celebrate my great affection for my colleagues in the Kennedy Center Opera House Orchestra to whom this book is dedicated.